THIS COLORING BOOK WILL SAVE YOUR MARRIAGE

A THERAPEUTIC COLORING EXPERIENCE

REYNOLD GREENLEAF

ISBN: 9781705610077

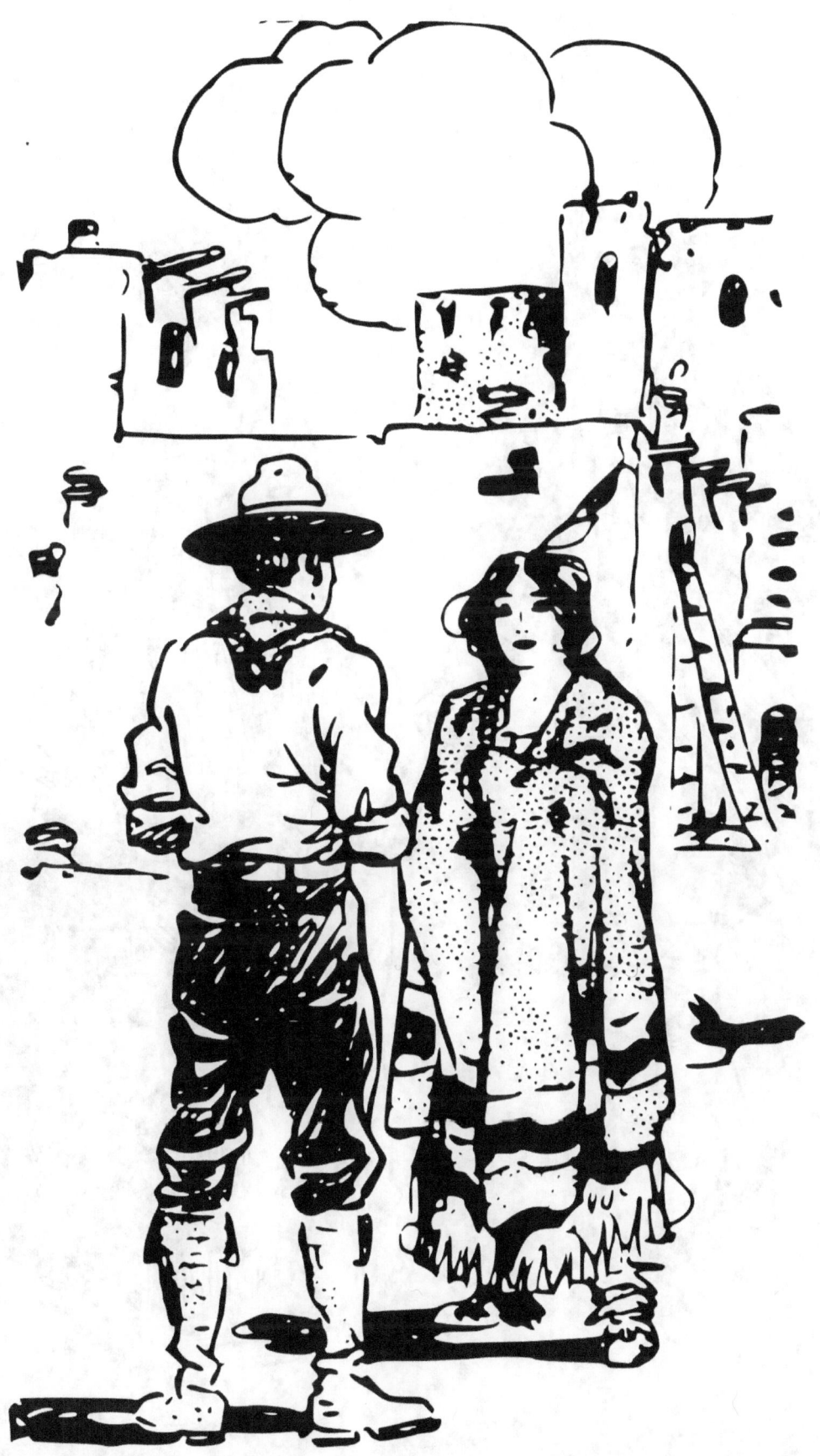

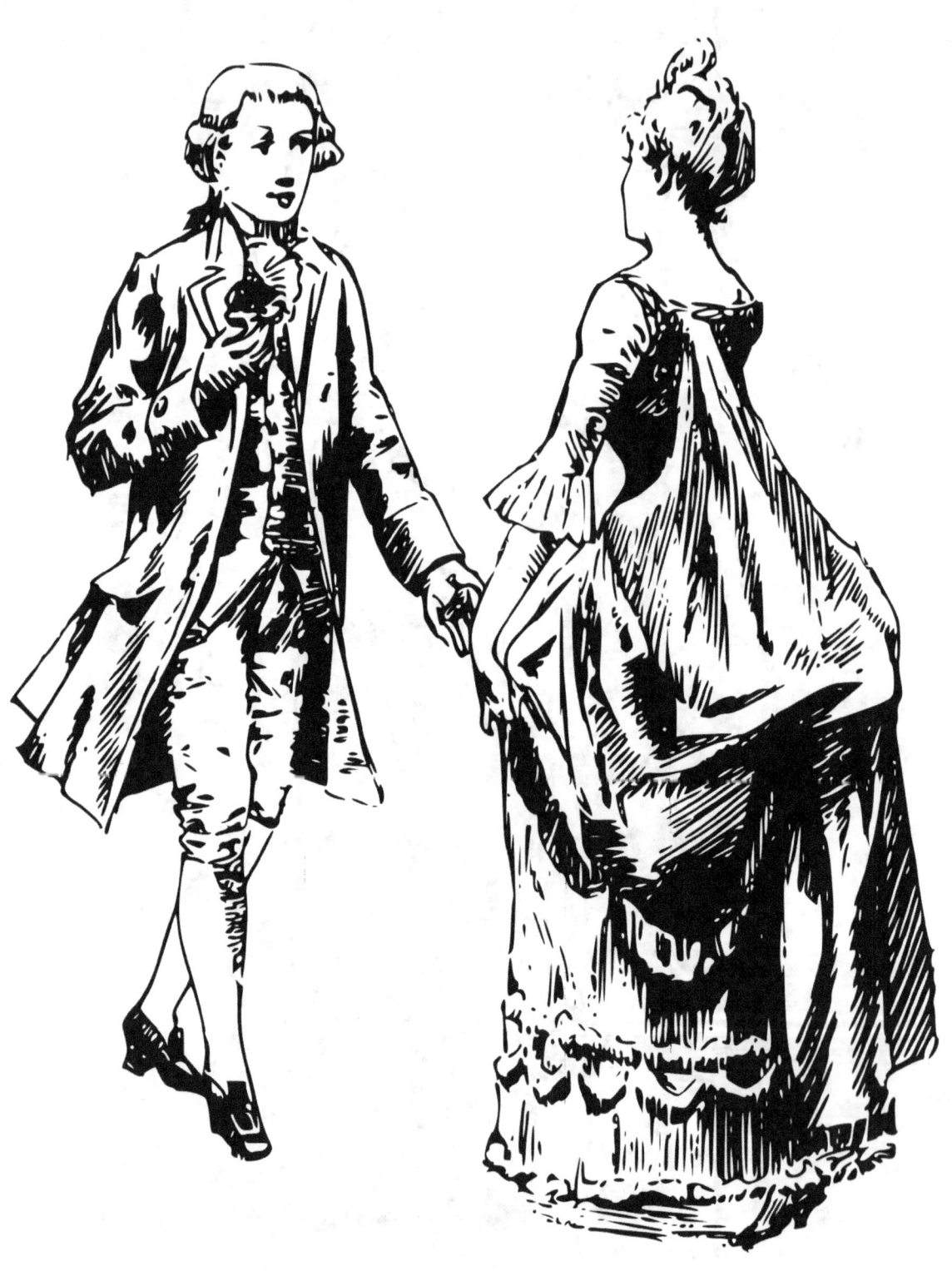

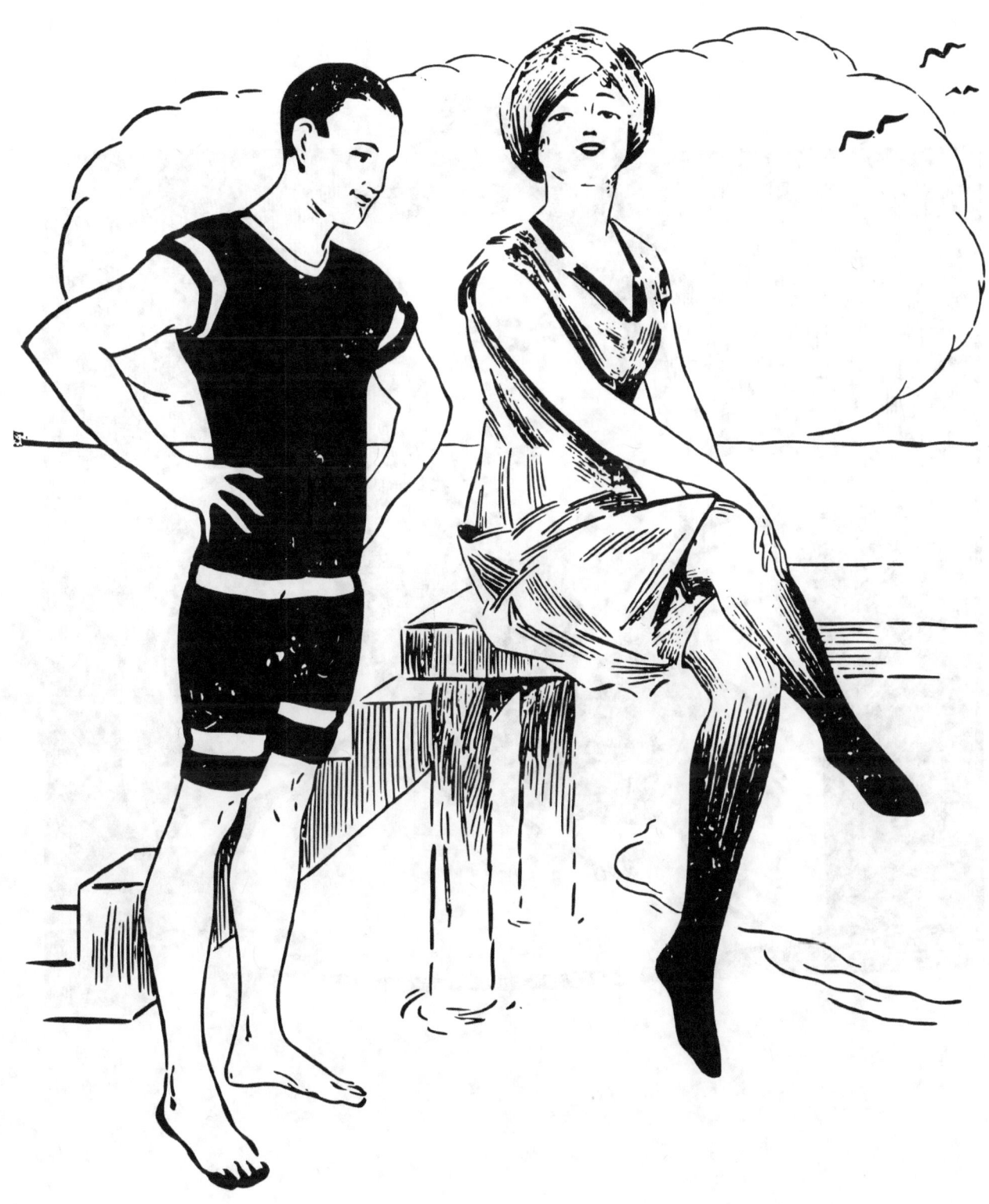

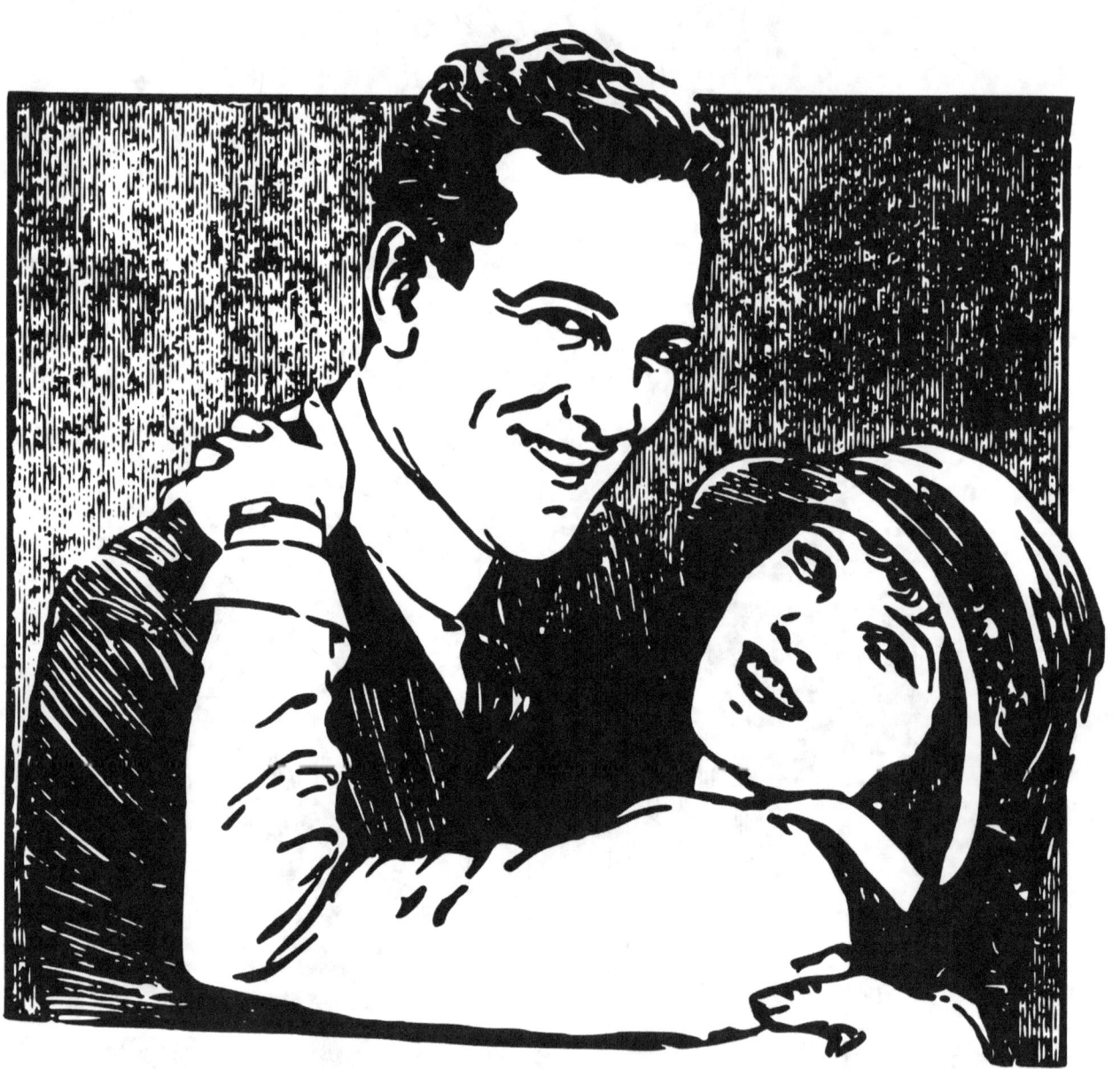

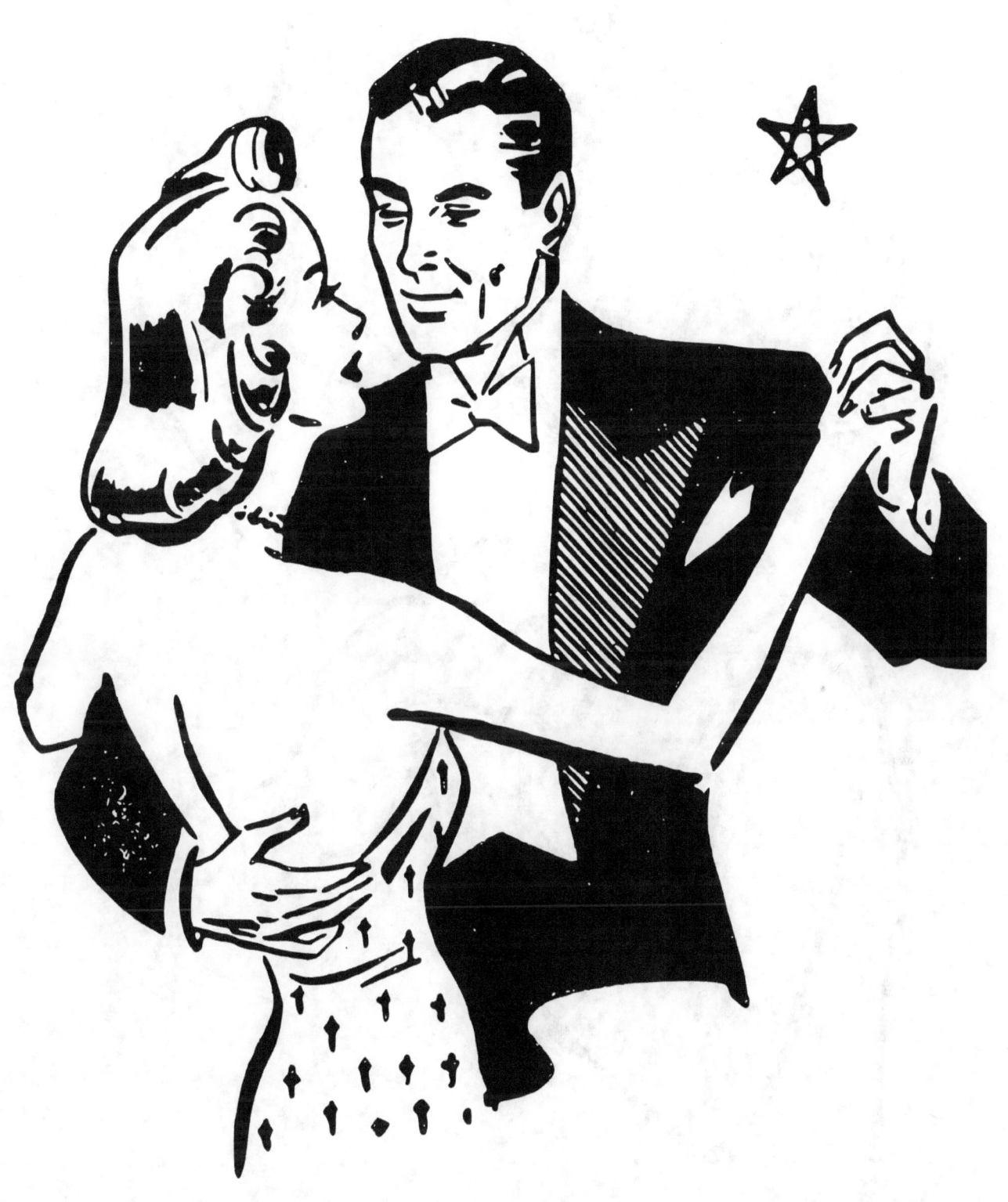

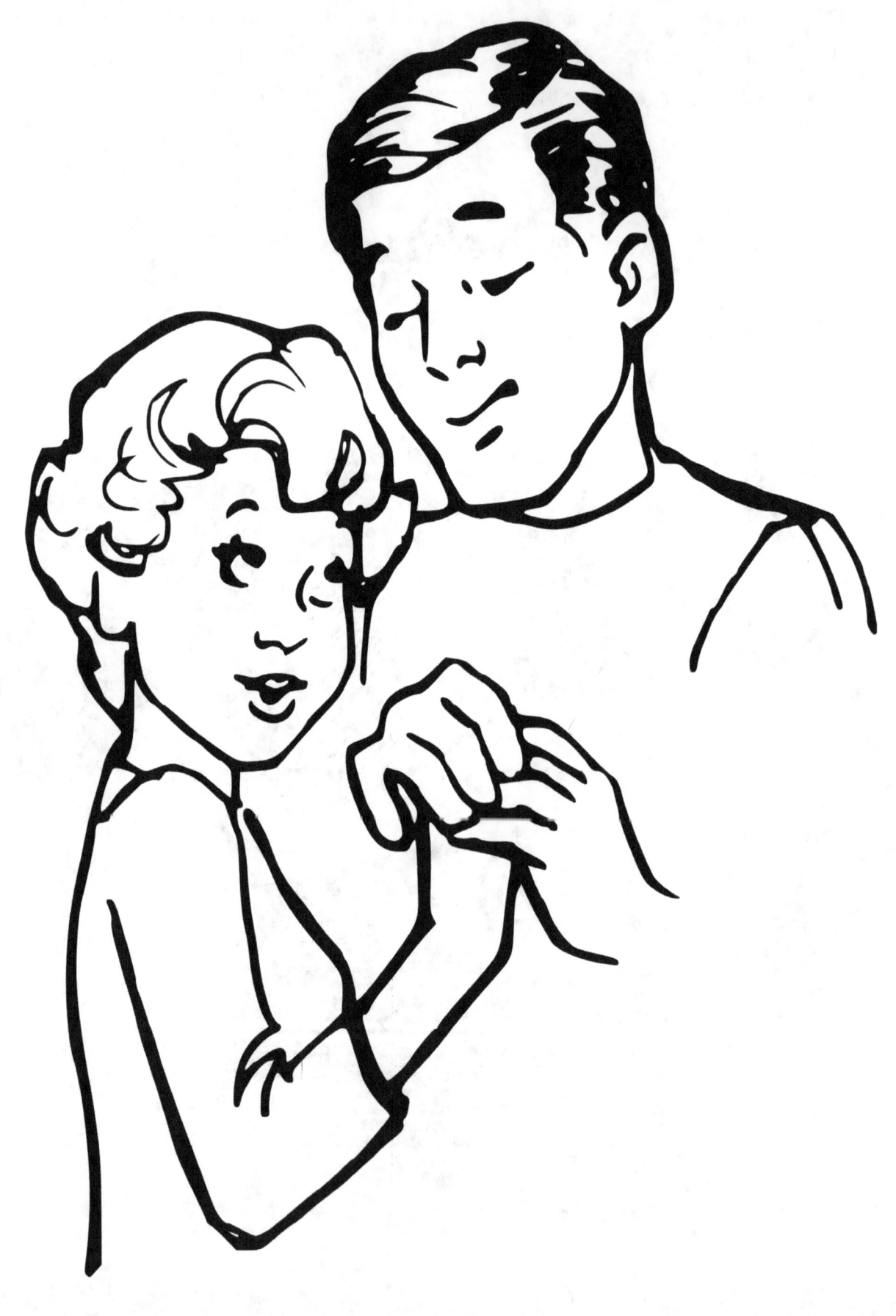

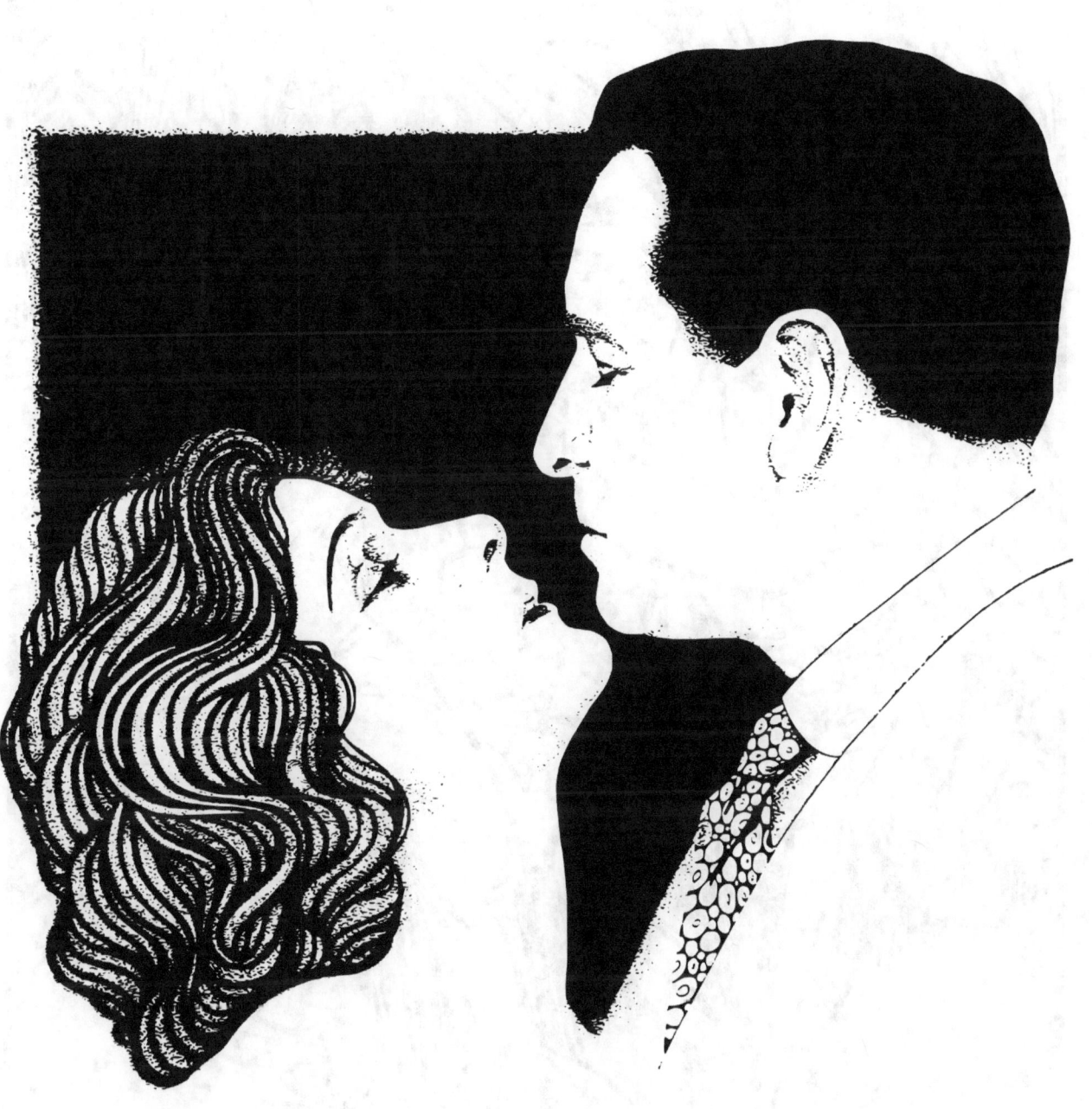

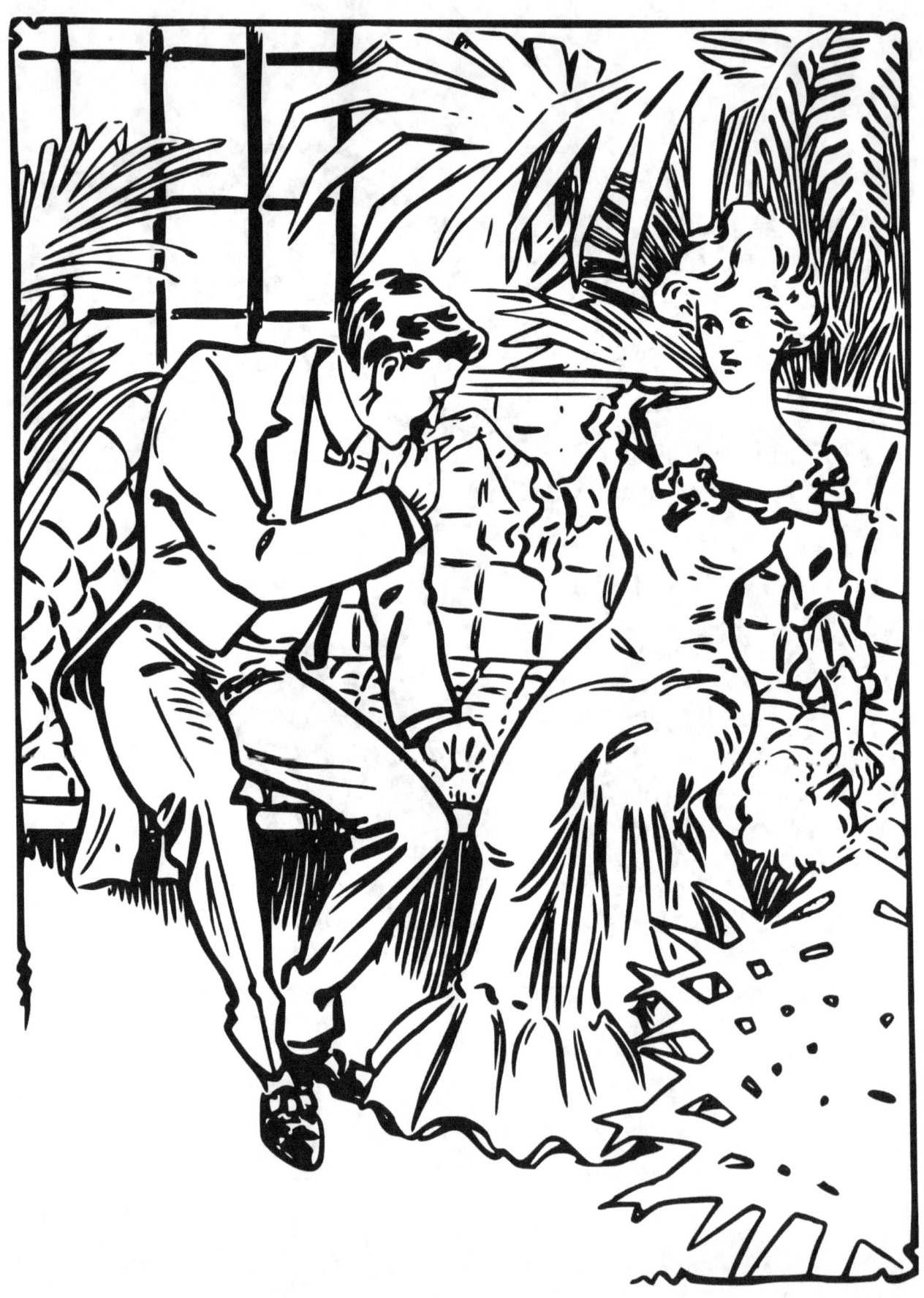

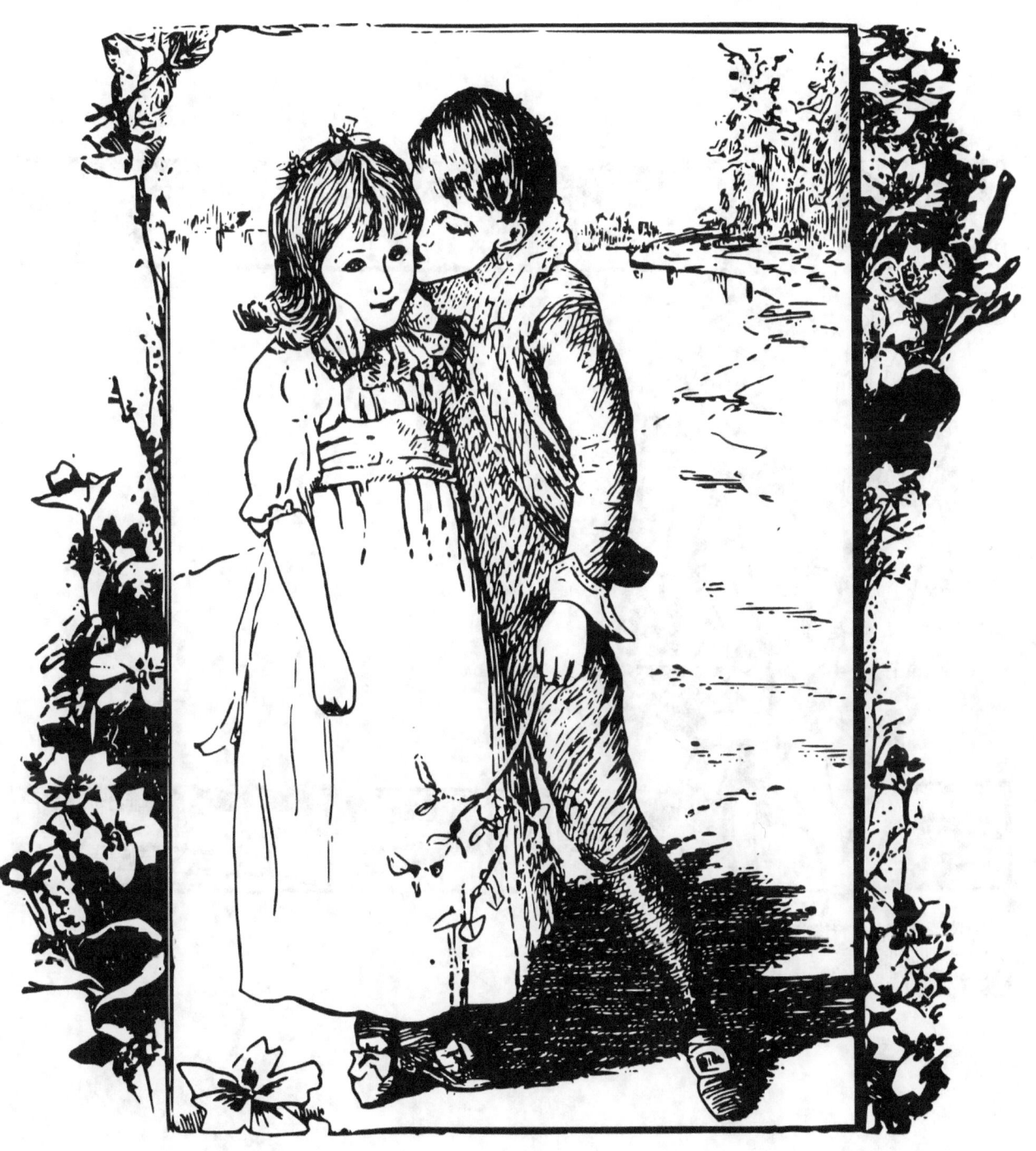

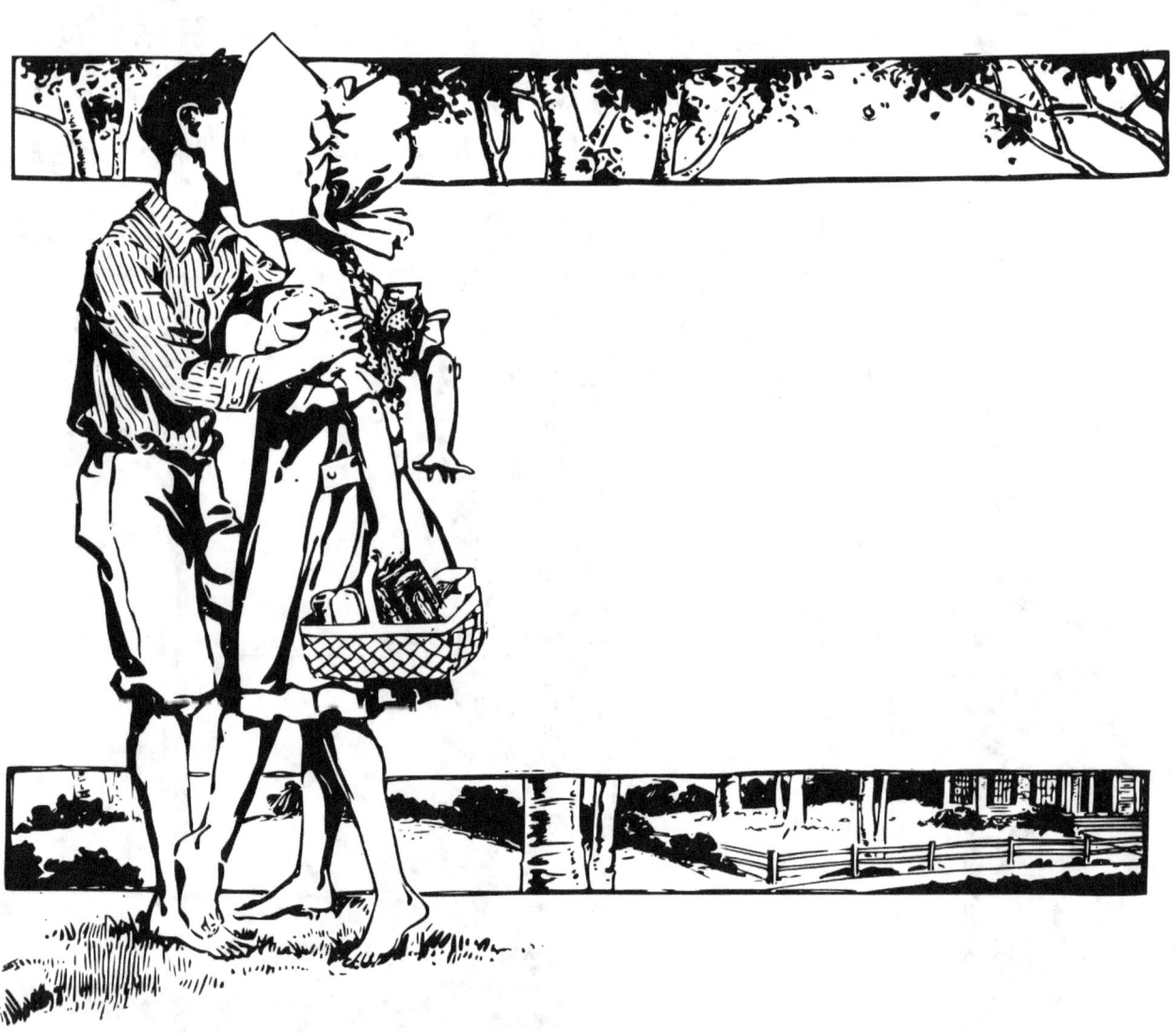

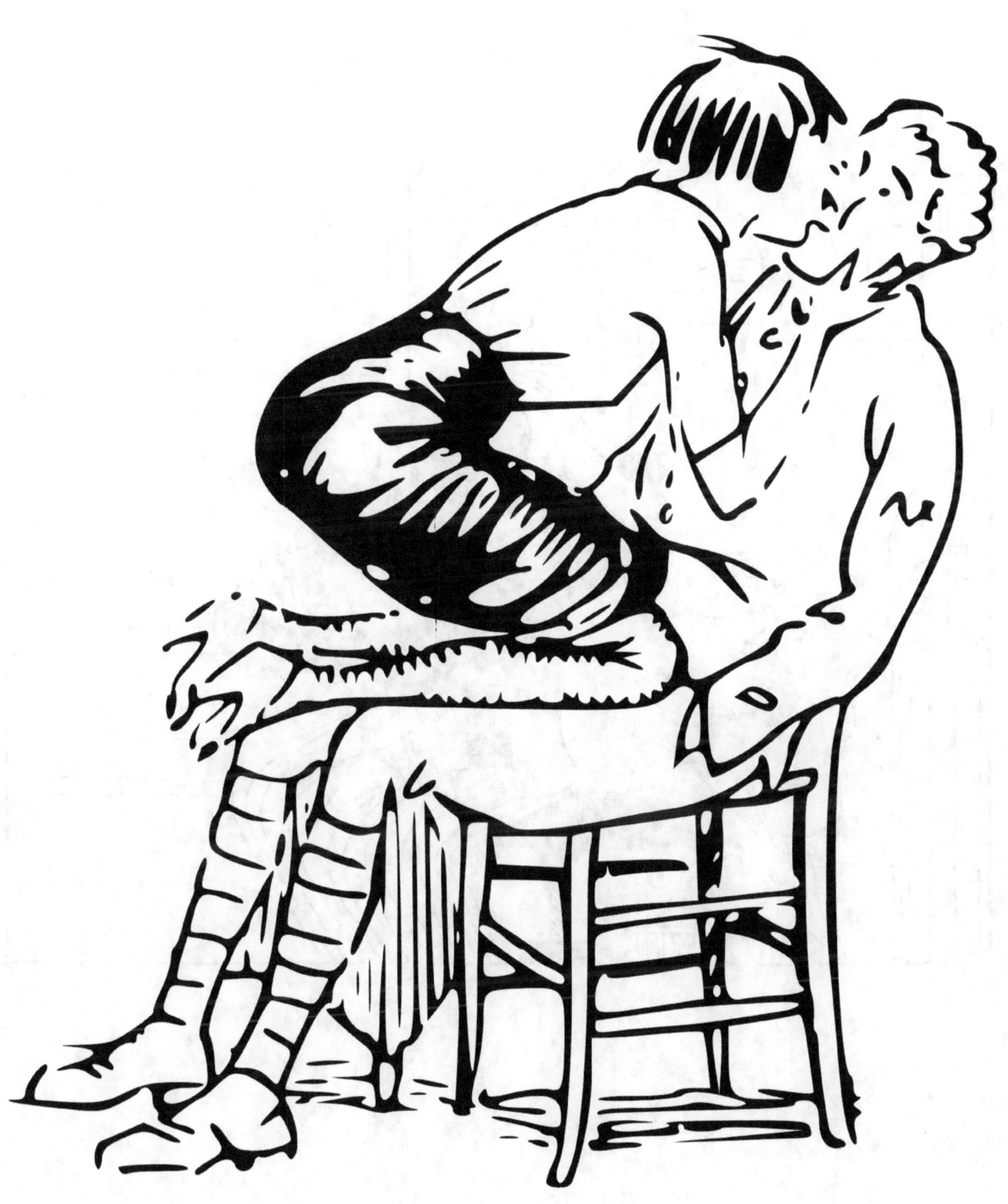

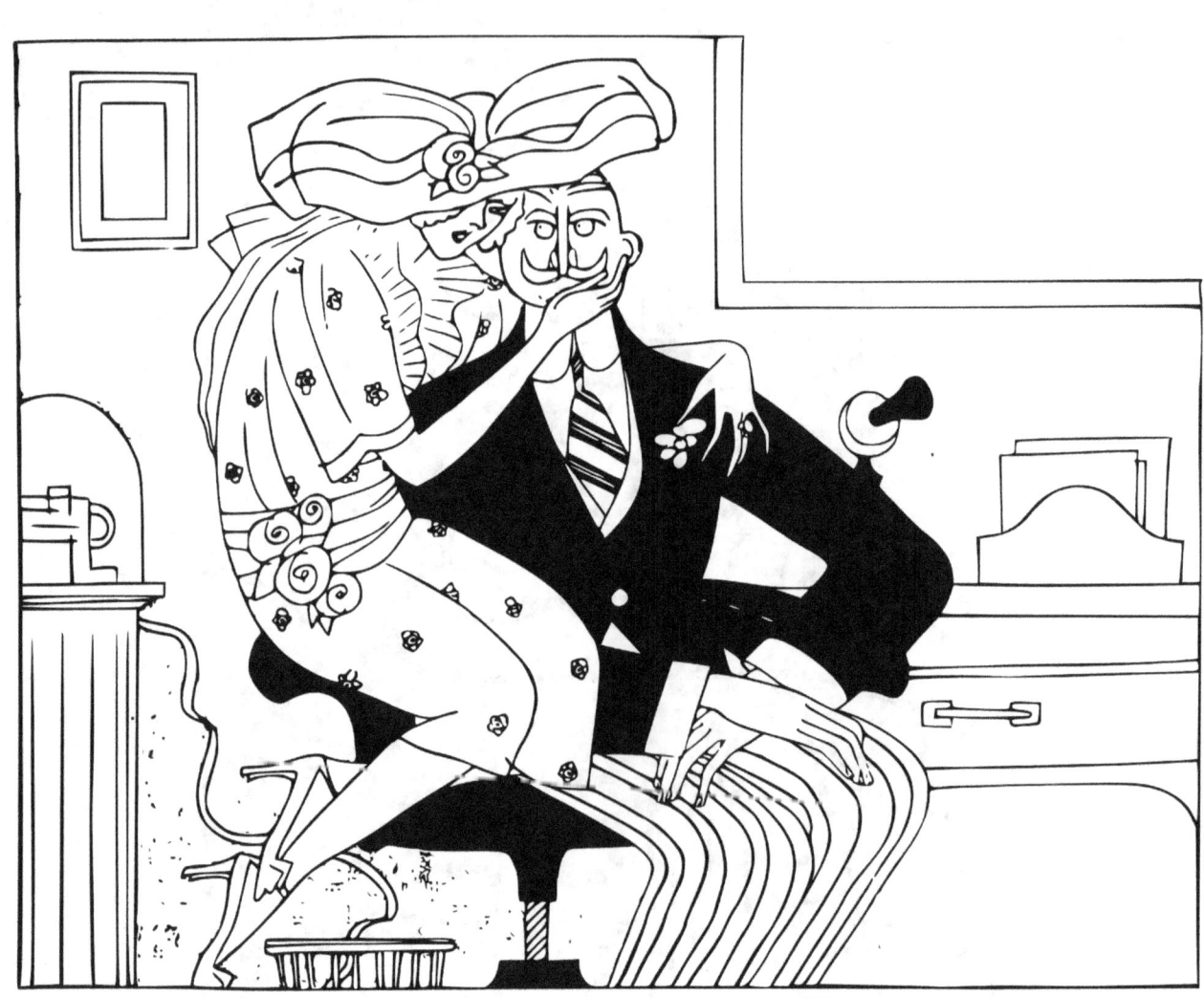

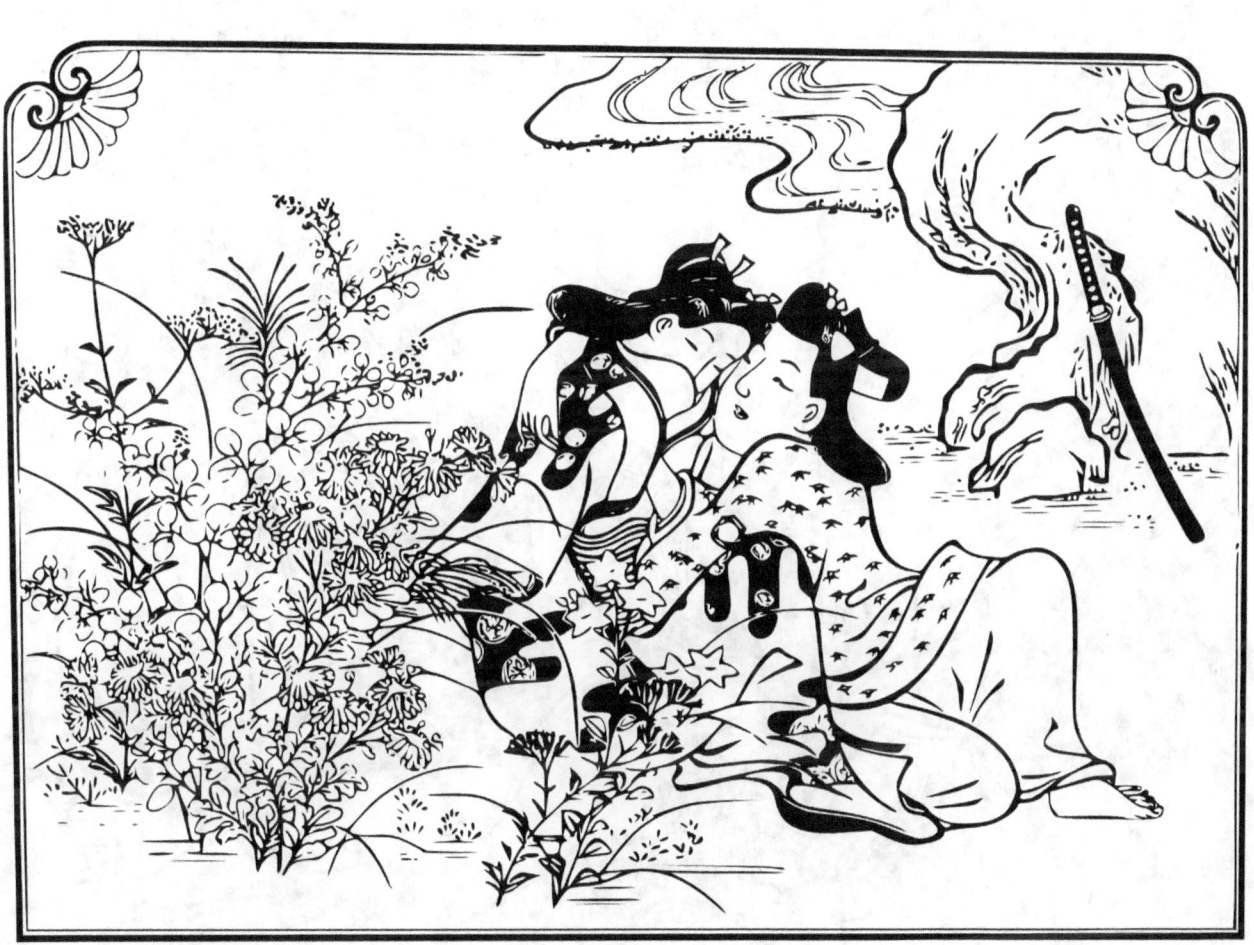

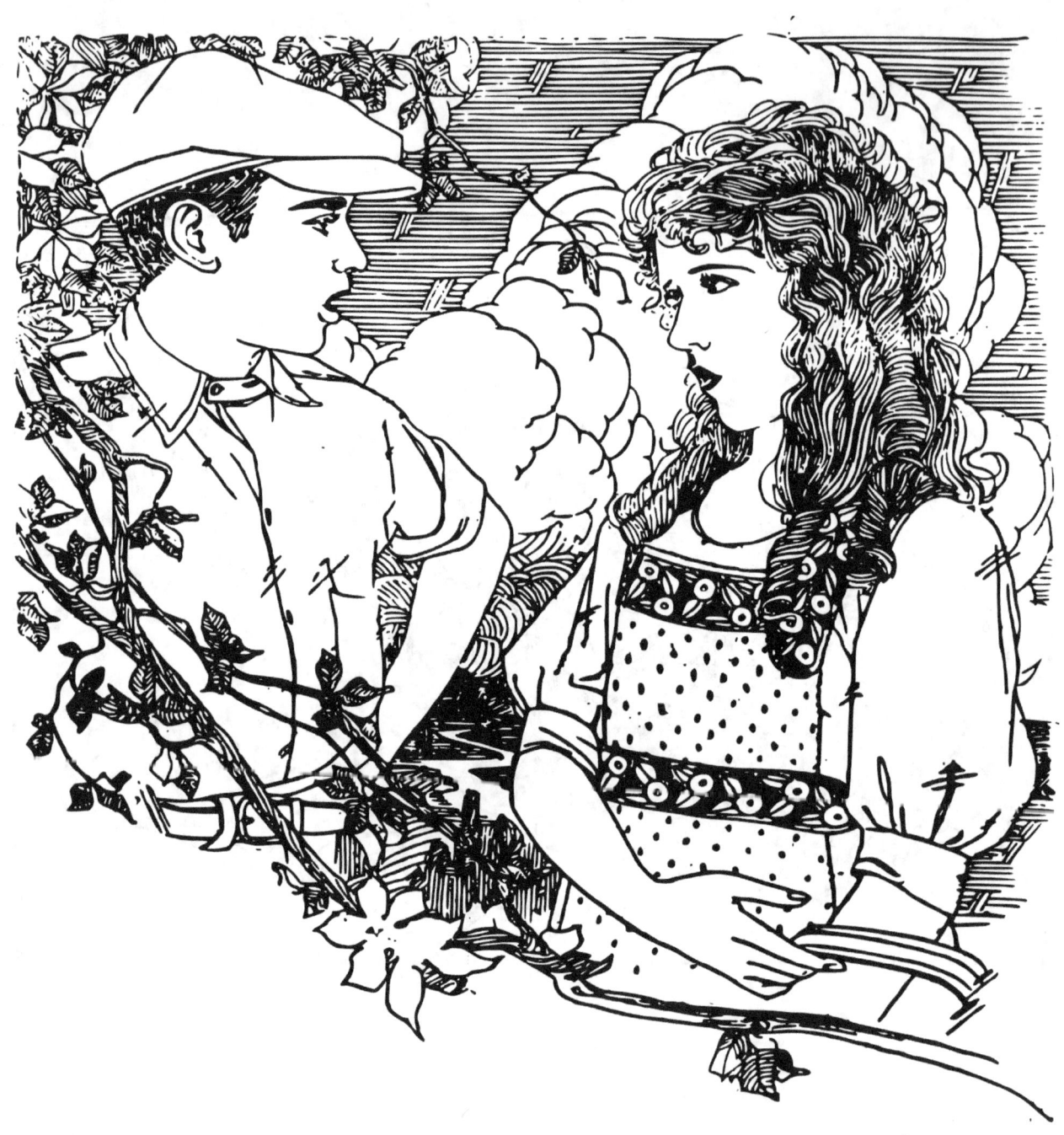

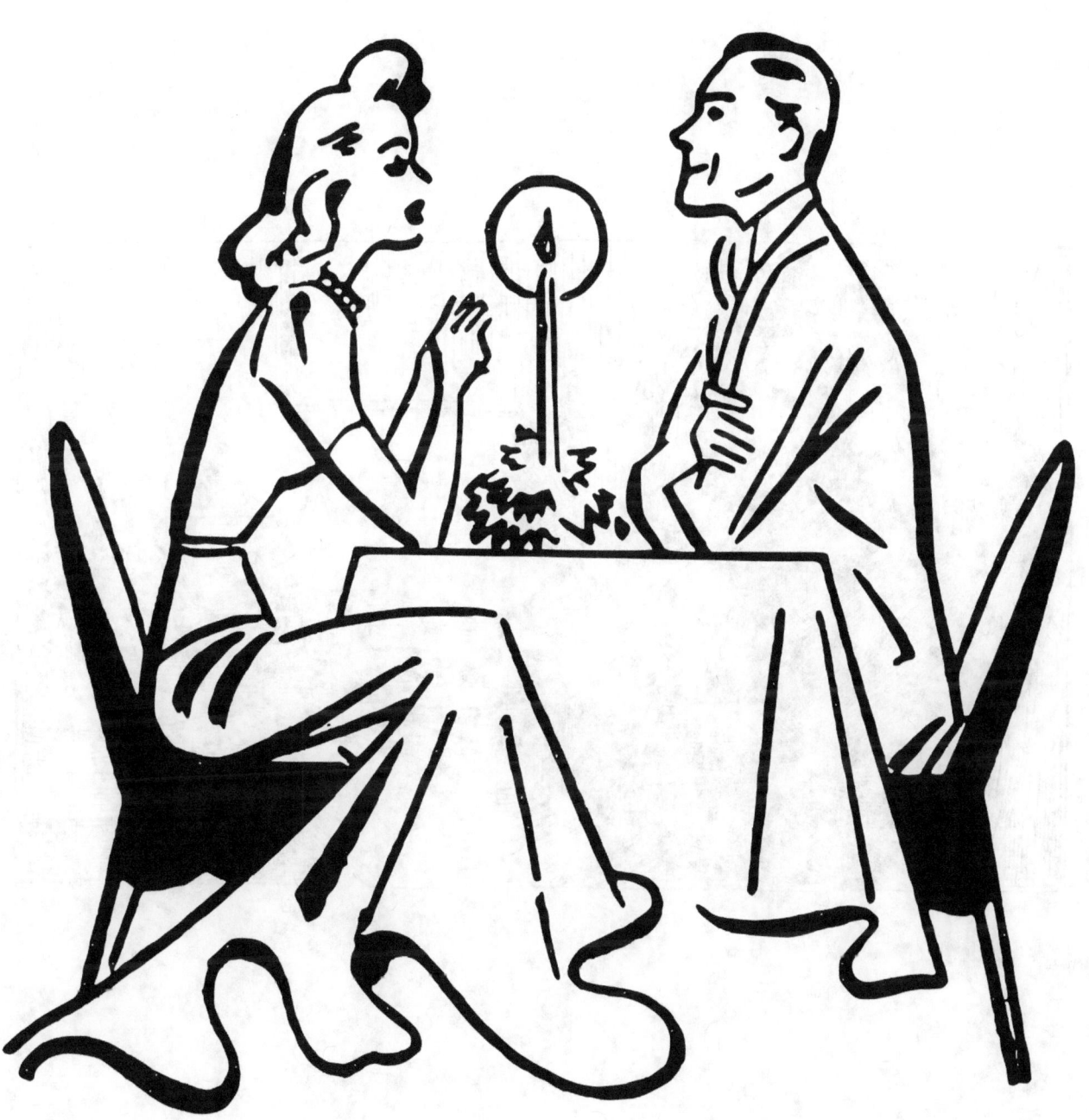

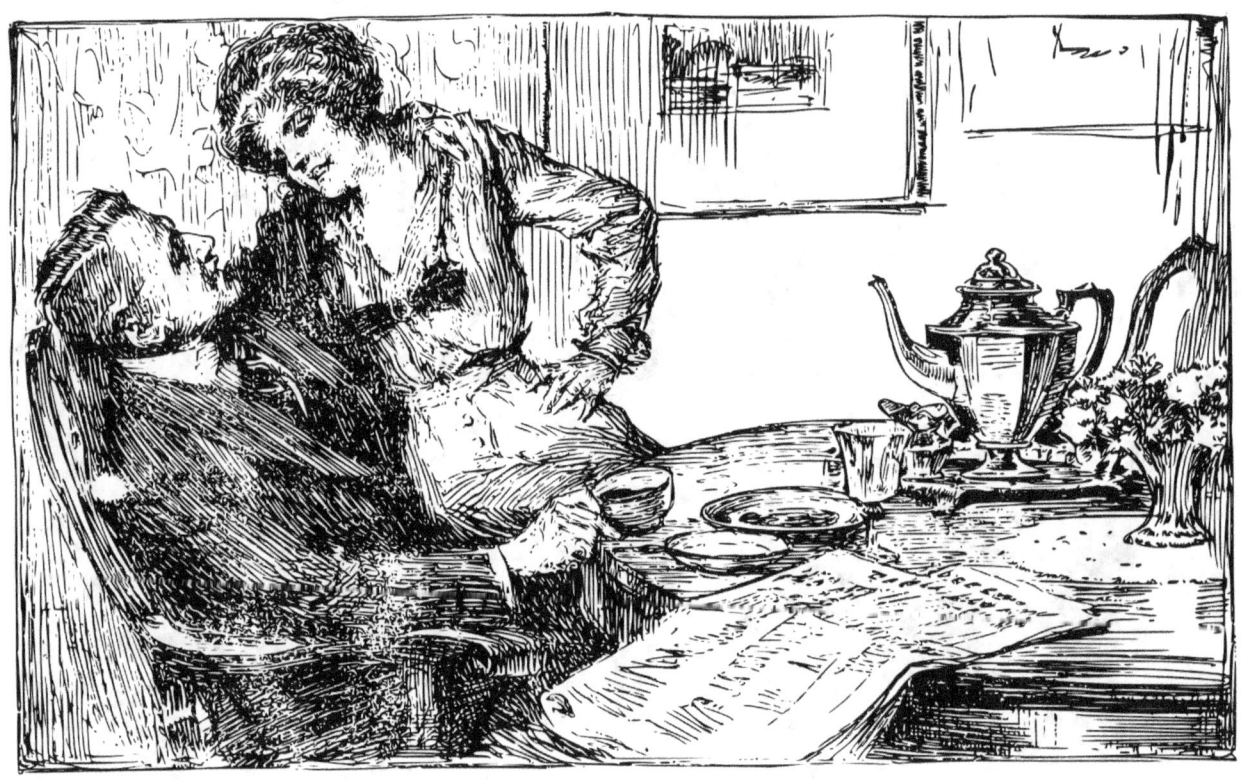

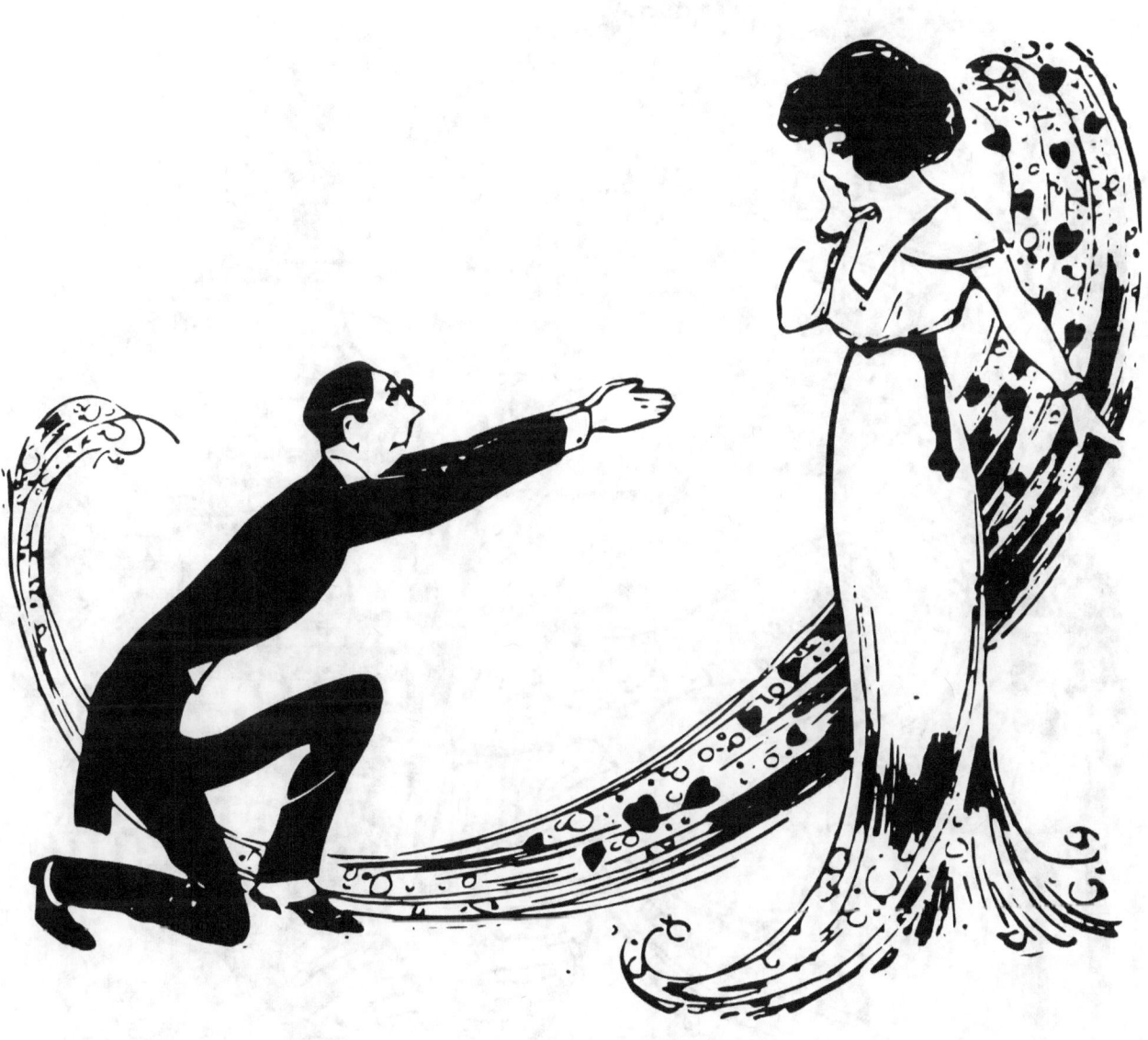

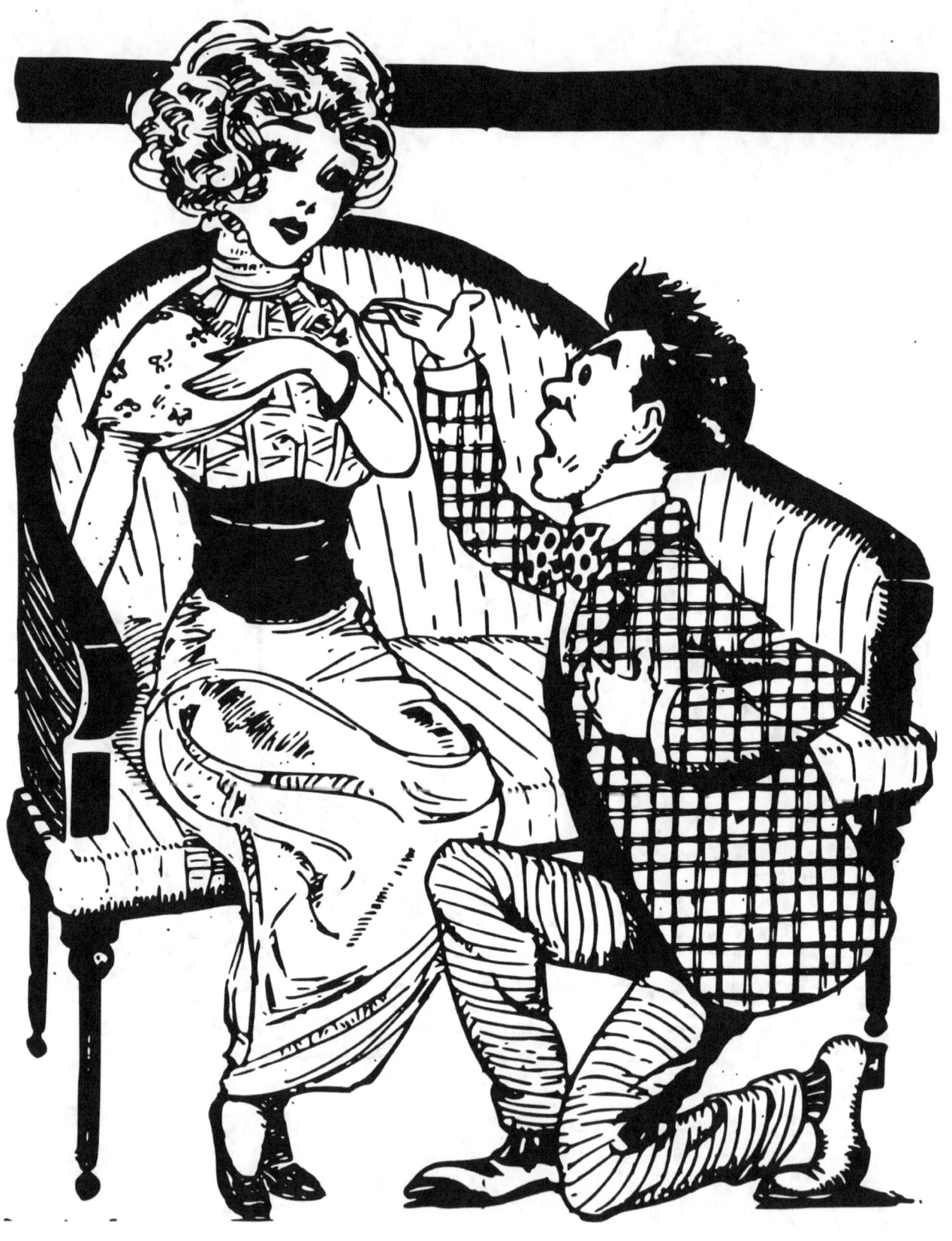

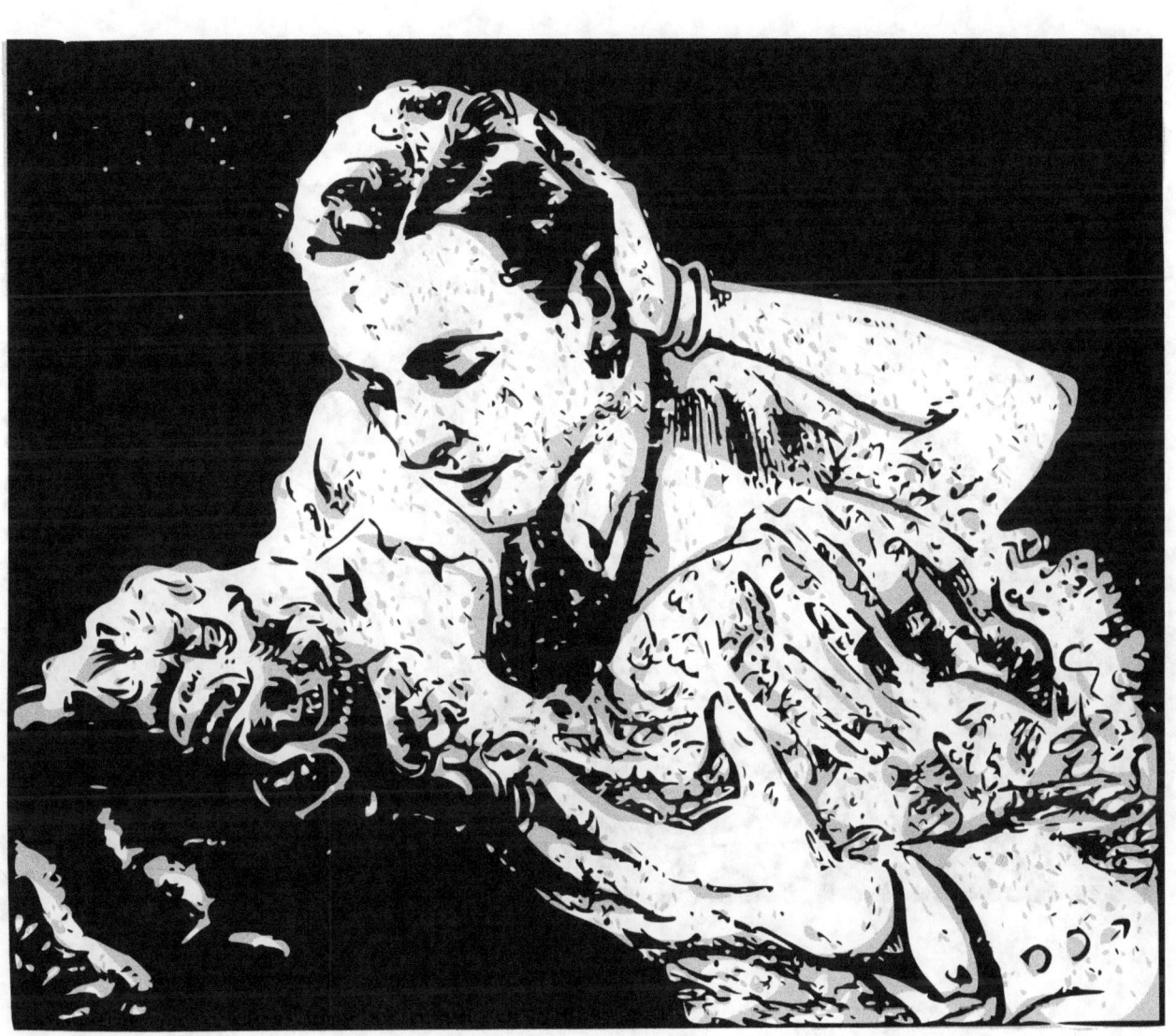

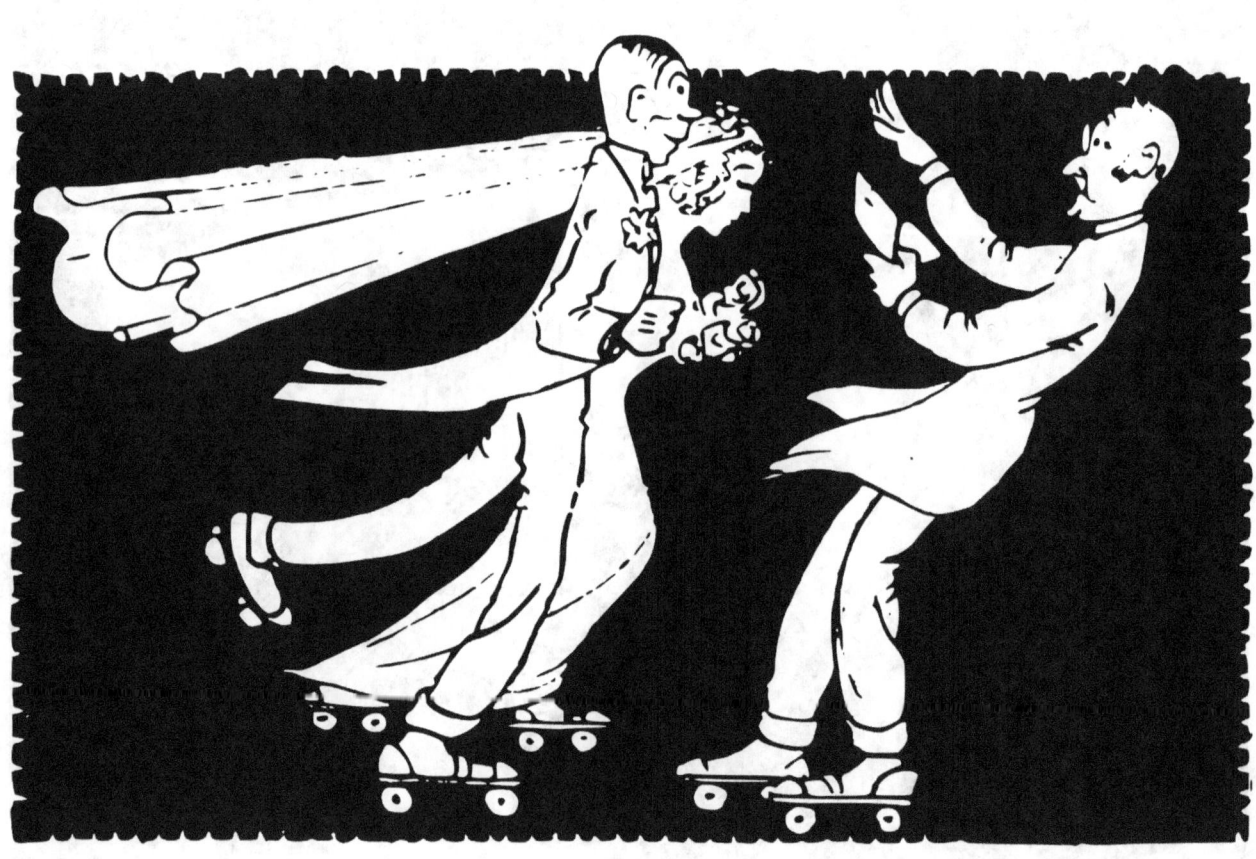

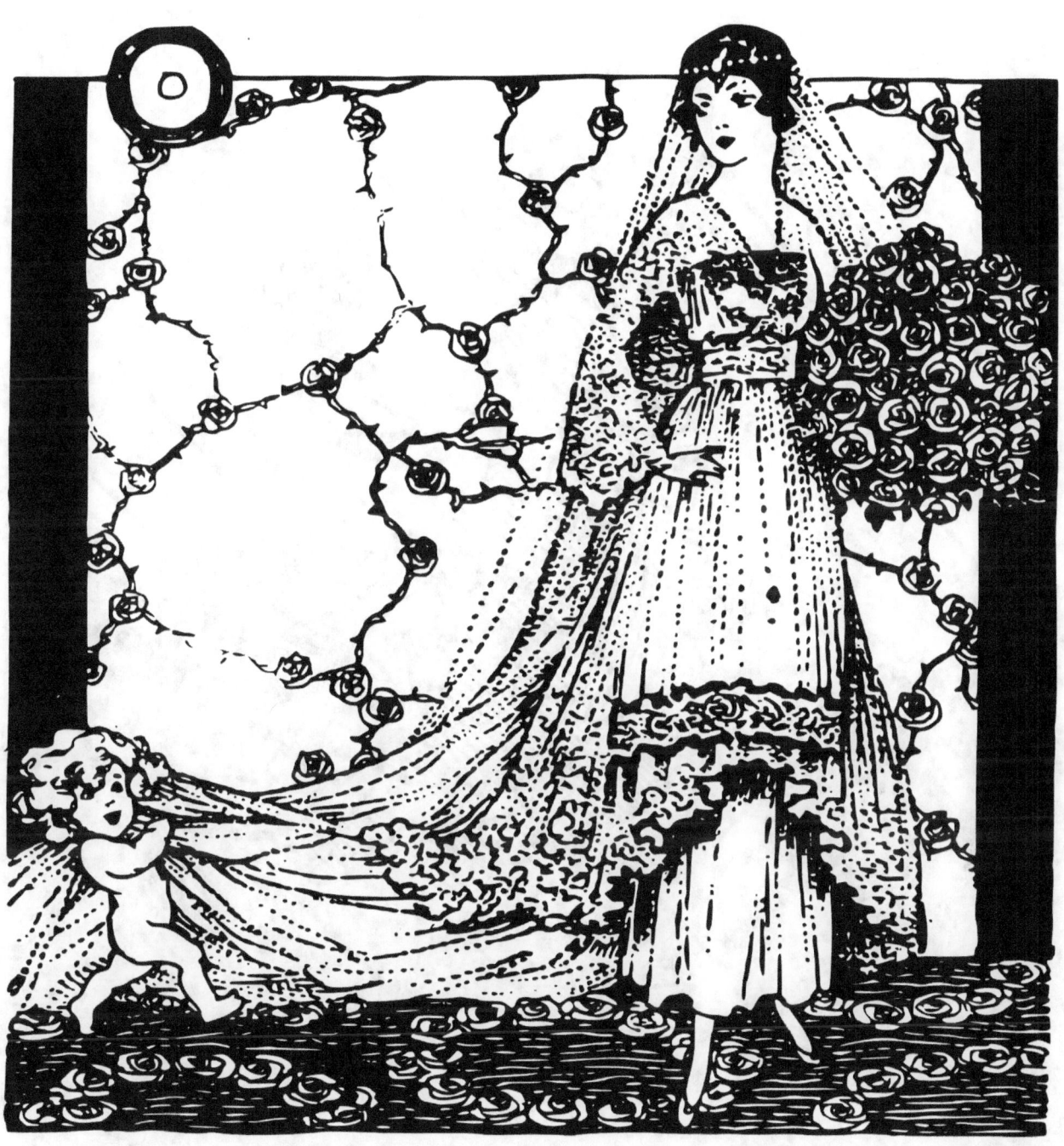

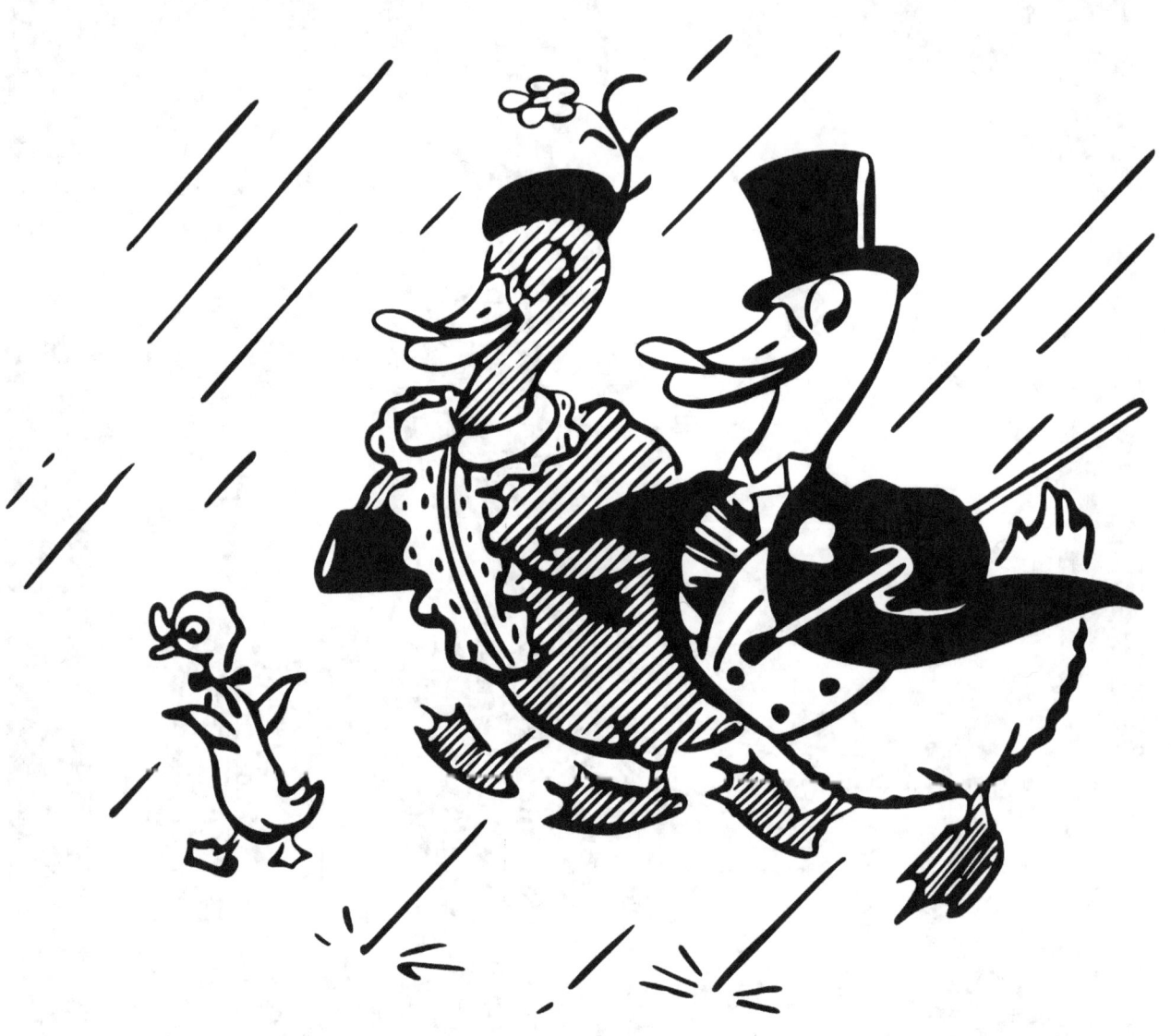

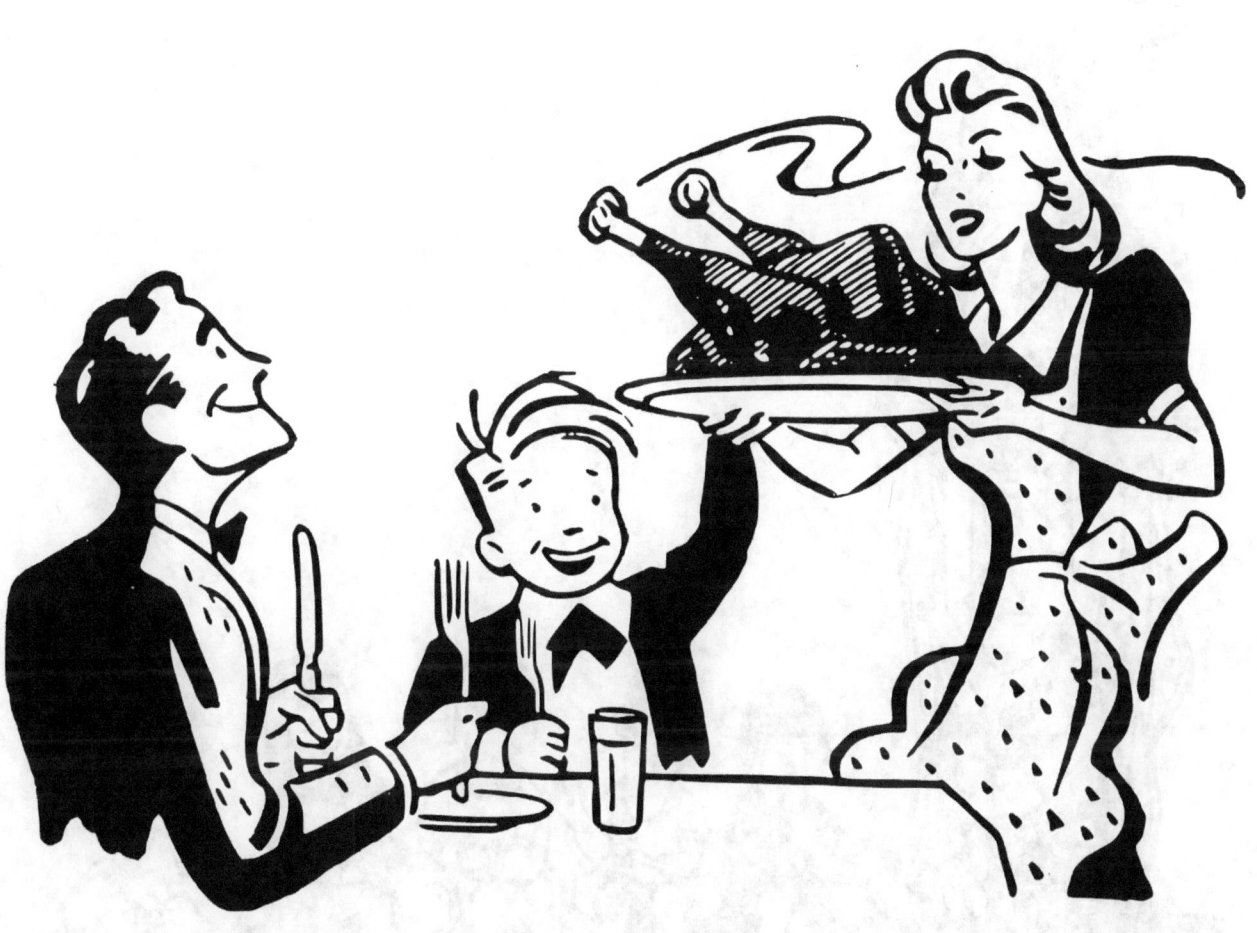

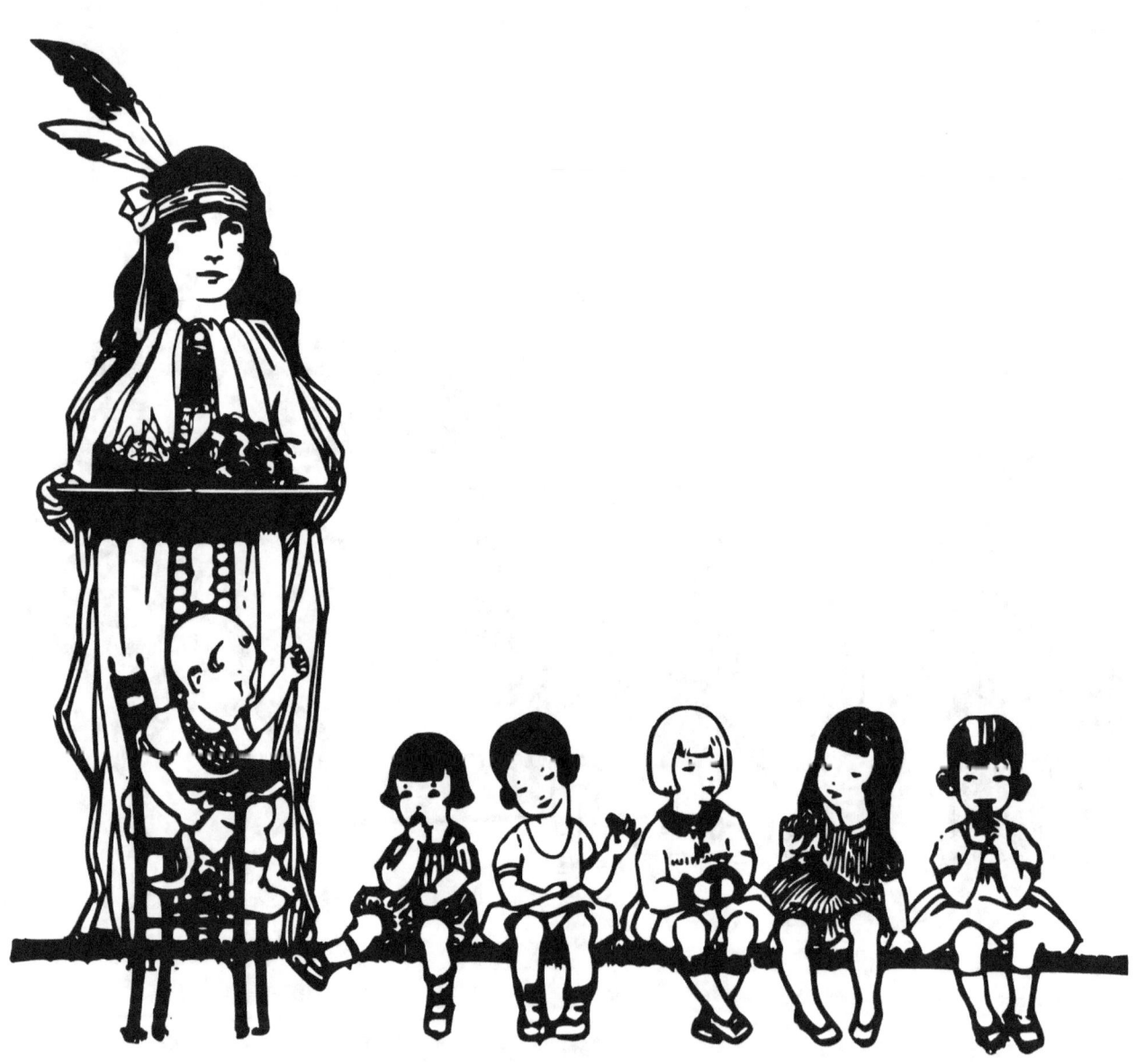

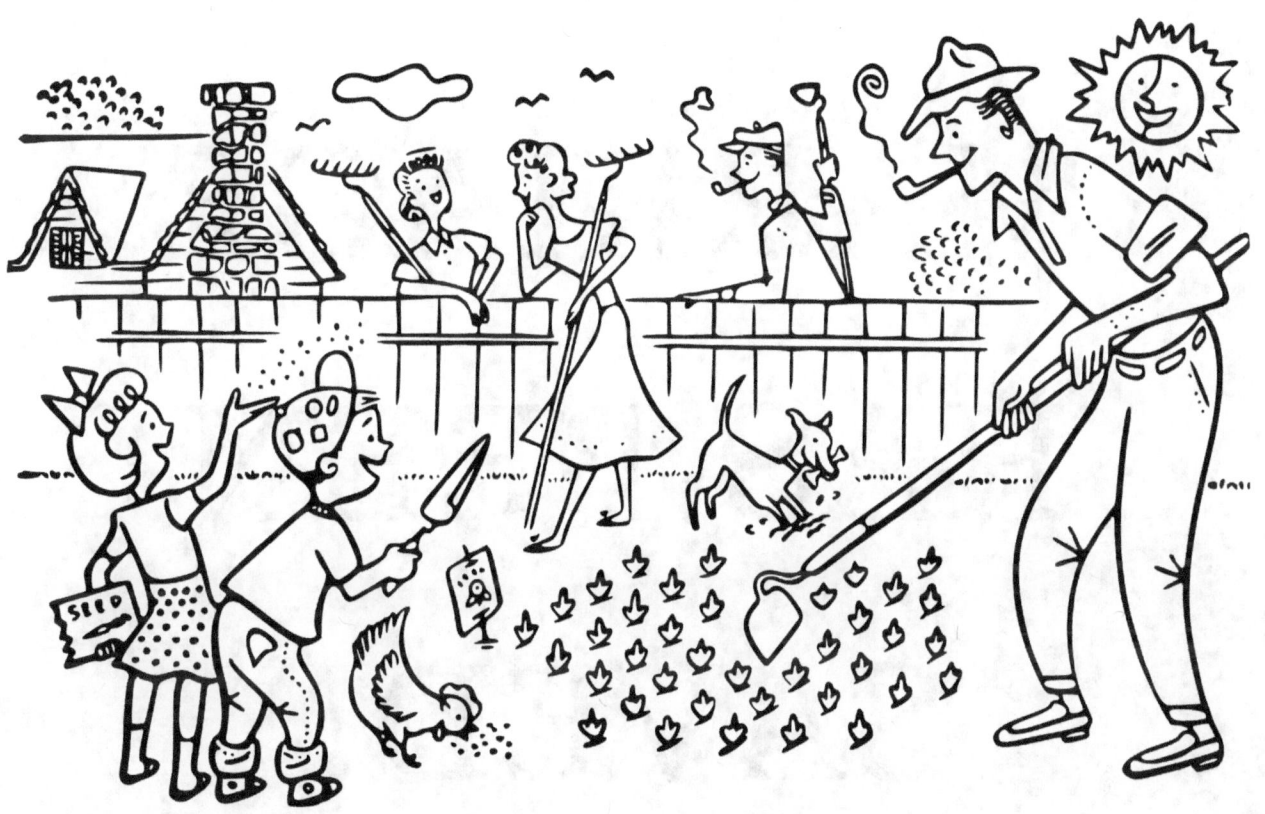

YOUR MARRIAGE HAS BEEN SAVED!

www.ingramcontent.com/pod-product-compliance
Lightning Source LLC
Chambersburg PA
CBHW082150230526
45467CB00043B/2795